Motherhood:

Plot Twist

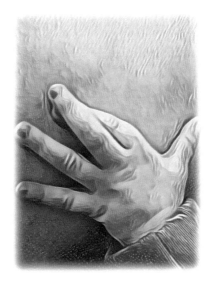

Aisling Finn

CONTENTS

Introduction

Three years ago, we received news that our son had a rare disease. When your child has complex needs, you are catapulted into a world of professionals, hospitals and it is overwhelming. Completely lost and unable to communicate my feelings, I started writing again as a way of processing my ever-changing feelings that came with mothering with such a plot twist. I have left the poems in the order that they were written to show how up and down the journey is. I hope my writing will help you to know that you are not alone in any journey that has given your life a plot twist.

Aisling

Ramblings

'A cat sat on a mat.'

Did the mat know

That this cat sat on it?

Or did it know this simple sentence

Would be said a thousand times?

Did it give meaning to the mat?

Or the cat?

Rhyme is a funny thing

When putting your thoughts into verse.

What words/phrases will leave meaning

Will they rhyme?

Do they need to rhyme?

Our thoughts deserve that outing

Every once in a while

So please write,

Write them all down,

Maybe one day your words

Will be repeated a thousand times

Even if they don't rhyme.

Whispers

I hear those thousand whispers from my
ancestors,

They bring my thoughts and feelings to be.

Words that I cannot normally say,

They help me write them in this poem for you.

Please sit back and read them,

Sit with my feelings…

Thoughts and be…

You deserve to hear you aren't alone.

We are all battling something,

Your thoughts and feelings are important

To me…

So, sit a while,

Listen to them if must,

Sit a while with me.

And listen to these whispers,

That allow us to be.

The first week

'Your baby can't feed.'

Not the words a mother wishes to hear,

After 2 days of labour.

The rush of oxytocin is compromised,

'What do you mean?'

They tell me you are too weak,

Exhausted from the marathon,

You need sleep.

I'm passed the syringes and left,

Left with thoughts on why you are weak.

I know something isn't right,

I pick you up,

I hover my milk by your nose to stir you,

There's no response.

I start to believe that you are tired,

And leave you to recover.

Day 2 passes

Day 3…

All failed attempts at bringing you to breast.

You turn away,

And I wonder why.

I ask for more investigation,

'He's just exhausted.'

I now pump, feed via a cup every three hours.

You are getting weaker,

My questions are more frantic...

Note: We did eventually breastfeed and continued for 14 months. It took 16 months for a medical professional to listen to my instinct that there was something that needed attention.

The Diagnosis

Somewhere in this life,

A plan was set.

We didn't get a say,

We didn't even know the day.

That day when the plan became clear,

All our inner hopes and fears,

Spilled out over scans, tests and numbers.

I looked back at your smiley face,

As I was told that unbearable news.

It was said that God gives strong people the pain,

I'm not sure that's fully understood.

I know that pain brings you to places

That you never knew or wished to go.

Pain lives deep within me.

It's there when I wake up,

And it tucks me into sleep.

I look back at your smiling face,

I feel your arms around me,

I hear you say, 'I love you Mummy...'

Sometimes it's as if you know.

You are reminding me love is great,

And that your love can weaken this pain.

After

I cannot tell you how I feel
Times like these can take their toll
There is no time to wallow
Nor is there time to quarrel

Life stands still
Whilst we take each other in
You have been mine from within

I cannot tell you how we will do
Nor can I tell you where we will go
My trust is in you and your trust is in me

I am but here and no where
My eyes fixated on letters
My fingers tapping
Endless searches
No results
Being rare is truly special

No Dr. Google
No forums
Not even a hashtag
I look within
I trust my instinct instead

My child

I could not think of anything better
Than to stare at you
and admire you,
My creation.

You possess so many miracles
That the eye cannot see.
But we do, we see you.

Catapulted

There's a gathering in my house.

There's a physio,

An OT,

The health visitor dropped by,

And the learning nurse too.

Our house is no longer occupied

By us 4,

I'm having to open the door to all.

I feel like I could fall forward

Into God's arms

He'd catch me

I'm sure

Instead I quiver on the edge here

Stop and Stare

Stop and stare if you must,

The scream of frustration has caught your ears.

Stop and stare if you must,

The angst from my child has caught your eyes.

Stop.

And.

Stare.

If.

You.

Must.

My eyes have caught your stare,

My ears can hear your gasps,

I am helpless in this moment.

I quickly avert my stare back to my child.

He needs me in this moment,

To comfort him,

And reassure him

That he is safe.

He throws his arms,

His jaw is tight,

His eyes are lost in his frown,

He curls into a ball

On the ground.

My heart is tight,

I don't know what to do…

I've been here a hundred times,

But still, I don't know what to do…

Time passes,

Others have joined the stare.

He squeals,

He covers his ears,

He can't hear me whisper, 'It's ok.'

He's waiting for the storm to pass,

I'm silently praying for his safe return.

Pause

He cocks his head up to catch my smile,

I offer my hand and pull him up,

His face slowly relaxes,

His eyes return,

His jaw falls.

He throws his arms around me,

Squeezing me…so tight.

I take a deep breath,

Silently thanking God for the calm,

Then we walk on as the crowd of stares

disperse.

Too much

Can I just step outside?
No post to pick up
No letters to google.

Can I just step outside?
To listen to a silly story
To laugh about nothing,
To just live without this.

Despair

I've parked despair outside the door.

He comes in sometimes,

He's not a guest I welcome,

Nor is he well behaved.

Despair is the swarm of bees

Moving back and forth outside.

He tries to rush in when there's an opening in the door,

I cannot let him.

If I did, he would consume every part of me,

The sadness he brings,

The pain he inflicts, deep inside my chest.

My soul tries to shake him off, but he always wins.

Despair is not my welcomed guest,

Nor is he well behaved.

Sometimes he is weakened,

When I am feeling strong.

He cannot worm his way in,

Because I am armed.

Despair cannot handle this,

I can feel him lingering,

Just in case I fall...

Or cannot stand

after that phone call.

Despair can sometimes comfort me

In my disbelief of life.

He can almost hug me when I think of what may

come,

Does he know what is to come?

Or is he living in the moment?

Sometimes Despair cries out with me,

I hear his echo in my heart,

My soul shakes because his power is so strong.

I feel my face scrunching when Despair comes,

It's like I'm trying to picture him,

And make sense of his own despair.

Despair is not my welcomed guest
Yet he brings me comfort in it all.
He reminds me to grieve,
To let it all, just grab a tear and fall.

Crutches

I'm leaning on my crutches today,

Insta, Facebook, even WhatsApp have left.

My crutches keep me upright, just.

They hurt sometimes,

They even make me fall,

But my crutches keep me upright, just.

Today

Today you are going to get up

Move forward

Hug for longer

Dust away negative thoughts

Be more loving

You don't need to have a hard shell

You don't need to wallow

You need to love you more

Share your beaming smile

Take note of the blessings

Laugh a little while longer

Let that laughter echo

The professional

When you say 'emotional response'
My response is emotional.
When you say 'struggles to process'
I struggle to process your words.
I can't help but think,
When you say these words
That you have forgotten
This is my child,
Our feelings,
Our world.

I ask, is it me?
You talk about parenting style
I ask again, is it me?
My 'style'?
I don't have a style, I'm just a mom
Who two years ago heard hard news,
I do my best.
I try all the strategies

I'm sometimes lost,

I reach out for help

From you,

But you shut me down with 'parenting style'.

Trust…

It's hard to open our lives up to professionals,

I can count 6 already,

I don't have the luxury of getting to know you,

Yet, I let you in,

I talk about the tough days and hope for more of
the good days,

You sit there,

Look sympathetic,

And all the while, the notes read 'parenting
style'.

You are a professional,

You have your processes,

You look at many cases.

I too am a professional,

But I'm also a mom,

I don't look at many cases,

I look at my child.

I implement processes

All…the...time.

I stopped reading these 'styles'

A mother's instinct is stronger.

My child needs his mom,

He needs me to love him,

Bring him joy,

Take care of him.

He's not judging me on my 'style'.

The trust is gone,

I'm closing the door.

Lean on me

You are mine,

And I am yours.

I know your pain,

I feel your joy.

I don't feel your pain,

Yet my tears do.

I can't take this away,

I can't put a band aid on it,

All I can do is talk.

Advocate,

Ask for help,

Take help,

Read,

Reply to comments,

Find the missing jigsaw piece, maybe.

But know that I am here,

I am yours,

Lean on me,

As you are mine.

The therapy

If I tell you,

Will the hurt stop?

If I tell you,

Will I feel less alone?

If I tell you,

Will I panic?

If I tell you,

Will I feel lighter?

If I tell you,

What will you say?

If I tell you,

Will I cry?

Some days

Today
Everything fell.
I can't shake it,
It has got the better of me.
It is hugging me,
It is pushing me,
It is in my way.

'Have your symptoms got worse?
Over the week?
Or the month?'
'Some days', I say.

They say it's normal
'You are coping with a lot.'
'Your body is pushed.'
'You've done well to cope this far.'
'Thanks', I say.
What else is there to say?

Ode to the oat bar

I can't crash the car

In the name of an oat bar!

It's dark,

There are beams of lights,

My mind is frazzled,

As I hear: 'I WANT A SNACK!'

Echo from the back of the car.

My frantic search

(With my left arm) is in vain,

For I can't crash the car

In the name of an oat bar!

Your request is angrier,

Your stance is more stern,

Mummy needs to find this oat bar.

The passenger seat is full of coats,

Bags, and even wrappers of oat bars,

But no, my arm cannot find what you want.

I steer the wheel with my right hand,

Careful not to mount another car.

I give up.

I say, 'Mummy can't look now,

we'll look when we get home.'

But you are insistent for that oat…bar…

We pull up, it's pitch dark.

I glance to my side,

To see an oat bar.

All along,

The oat bar was in reach.

Yet, you don't care,

As you have found Daddy's car.

Your need for the oat bar is no more.

Now mummy can relax

Knowing that I didn't crash the car

In the name of an oat bar!

Losing Mummy

She's forever losing something,
Her glasses, her keys, even her cup of tea.
Sometimes I hear her mutter words to *St*
Anthony,
Sometimes I hear her get frustrated,
Other times, she just cries.

She says it's because she's tired,
If only you kids slept,
Gave Mummy some rest,
To find the glasses, the keys and even the cup of
tea.

Prognosis

Live for a better day.
You must live
For a better day.
Live for
A better day,
You
Must
Live
For *another*
Day.

You must live for the day in it,
For the day is what you must live for.
The day you keep hoping for,
That day will come,
Only if you live for that day.

The switch

'Too wet

Too hard

Too soft

Too…

Too…

Too…

Too…

Yucky.'

Burnout

I've hit a wall,

I can't take another head butt from hunger.

I can't take another kick into my shins.

I can't even heave the load up anymore.

I'm tired.

I'm tired of explaining,

Repeating myself,

Tired of asking for support,

And tired of having no response to my cries.

I want to move past these things,

My mental energy is depleted,

My body isn't doing what I want it to do.

They say here take this, this will help you along,

All I see are risks

With just taking this.

What if I get ill?

Who will take the load then?

Who will make sure things tick along?

Who could replace me?

All I want to do is stop this feeling.

But like the others, it's just hugging me,

And it won't let me go.

Loss

When I think of loss,

I can't breathe.

No counting in for 4….

And out for six……

There's a fear inside me that will not go,

No amount of therapy or doses will remove this.

It's whirling around on its own,

Like a child spinning around.

Except there's no laughter here,

Just dreaded fear.

It is heavy,

Pulling me down.

The Hospice

It rained heavily that morning,

Dark, cold and a feeling of dread,

And maybe apprehension.

A rushed breakfast,

30 minutes late,

We arrived to a little building that had a sign

nearby that read, 'Baby Hospice'

Opening the door to a glow of yellow,

A nurse warmly welcomed us in.

It slowed my racing heart,

Eased my frown,

And I felt at home,

Just as I wanted you to feel.

Gazing at pictures of past patients,

Wondering did they go on or were these the
smiles of past?
A reminder to myself of where we were,
Why we were there,
Another experience to recall.
Another experience that will tell all.

A message from a friend later that day,
She knew what to say,
How to acknowledge this new experience,
She simply said, 'Well done'.

The pain

The pain creeps in

And catches me unawares.

There's no 'start' button

Just a crashing wave.

I can feel the depths of that pain

It consumes all of me.

I try to reason with it

Send it on its way…

But my subconscious mind

Knows that this pain is here to stay.

Thank you

If today you have shown me kindness,

I thank you.

If today you saw that my lip curled when I said I
was okay,

I thank you.

If today you pretended to believe me when I
said last night was easy,

I thank you.

No doubt last night I picked up a few more
fears,

Not from Dr. Google, but from other avenues.

Avenues in my mind that lead to 'fatal' or
'progressive'

My mind isn't free from any fear,

There's sometimes logic but mostly it's heart
wrenching fear.

How will I prepare?

What will it start off as?

Is there treatment?

Is there going to be more pain?

I thank you.

Dear Teacher...

Dear Teacher,

Whilst you sat and turned away to list the flaws

in my child,

You shattered my hopes.

Our child,

Carries a big weight with her every day.

She can't name it,

She can't see it,

But she'll get anxious.

She will probably 'annoy' you.

She's panicking inside,

She has a lot to deal with.

Her peers don't deal with what she does,

You do not deal with what she does.

She's chatty, yes

She's busy, yes

But she's not 'annoying'
She's not all the things you said she is.

She's very caring,
She helps her brother do lots of things,
She's the reason he can do lots of things.
She's a force of nature,
An 'old soul',
Call it what you like.
Some even say a 'pocket rocket.'
But she is certainly not 'annoying'
She is just 6 years old,
Living through a pandemic,
As a young carer.

Ode to my daughter

Did I tell you about the brightest star?

She loves fiercely,

She looks beyond the emotion,

Brings you a tissue,

Wipes your eyes,

Breathe in mummy, breathe out.

She takes everything in her stride.

Her soul sees beyond your comments,

Yes, she's loud,

Yes, she's assertive,

But she too hurts easily.

I hurt easily when you diss her presence,

She's not bossy,

She's not rude,

She's living her life, unapologetically.

She's caring towards your children,

She hugs them like there's no tomorrow.

She wipes their tears,

She holds their hand,

Whilst she encourages them to try

Rather than quit.

My child may be spirited,

But it's not a bad thing.

She is the brightest star,

And I am proud of her.

Night watch

Waking up to check you,
Pangs of pain in my head,
Still tired from checking you
From the night before.

You are softly sleeping,
My eyes can't see you breathe.
A moment's panic washes over me,
I can't rush in,
So instead I swiftly move
…closer to hear you.
Then I see your tummy rising,
All is well, I say.
Then I look at you and wish this was
Not happening to you.

You lie beside me,

You have already insisted a light be on.

Mummy's eyes are fixated as you gaze on me,

You whisper, 'I love you Mummy, you are the best.'

Then you drift

Off to sleep,

Safe with mummy too.

The one that got me

My heart is thumping listening to those lyrics,

Analysing which parts weigh heavy on my soul,

on my body…

'May you stay forever young.'

Songs sung with soul smash through all coping

strategies.

The tears are falling,

I don't want to stop listening.

I want to feel through the music,

Let it go through every part of me.

I want my body to remember this feeling,

It's complete lack of control over emotion.

Like it's ok to fall victim to that,

It's what makes us mothers, fathers and alike.

How could anyone not feel this loss?

I best get up

I best get ready

I best give the doses

I best give time

I best give play time

I best give hugs

I best give kisses

I best look together

I best look happy

I best look pretty

I best tidy

I best clean

I best dust

I best feed

I best get clothes ready

I best pack everyone's things

I best put everyone to bed on time

I best get everyone up on time

I best pack the car

I best give everyone a memorable holiday

I best not to forget me.

Lingering

I could be stood making waffles,
When I catch a glimpse of a smiling face on the
windowsill.
A reminder of how far we have got together,
Then my emotions are catapulted back to those
words, indescribable and so painful.

Please don't call me strong

My days cannot be compared to a weight
bearing,
There's no one else here.
I can't hear puffs of breath as one lifts a heavy
load,
All I can hear is Mummy, over and over again.

Little marks from constant pushing,
I'm your safe place,
Like a bean bag.
Yet, my skin isn't cloth,
It bruises easily,
With little 'I love you Mama' (s).

Calling

My hands have barely touched this mug of tea

Before I am called for again.

This time it's because someone forgot to adjust

the seat for you.

I mutter to myself again to remind the

household once more,

Just so I don't have to keep on getting up.

You say, 'Thank you Mummy.'

I linger for a little while,

In case you need me again.

You are so happy with yourself,

This piece of independence means a lot to you

and me.

I was right, you do need me once more.

You wash your hands and go off to play,

I sit back down to my mug of tea which is now a

little cold.

But the seat is adjusted with your step and all,

so you don't have to call for me.

Time

Time isn't to eat,
Maybe a drink of tea
Or milk.
Wine helps drown the pain out,
Wine also helps you to speak what you can't
say.

Time is spent questioning,
Listening to the saddest music,
Feeling the sadness with others,
Helping time pass.

Can time stand still?
Are we running to just stand still?
That next letter, next phone call, next
appointment
Talk about it all over again and again and again
How many more times do I have to relive that
day?

How many more times do I have to explain?

How…many…more…times?

Angst

I just can't bare this feeling,

It takes up all of my heart.

The pain, the thoughts, the what ifs,

It will never diminish.

It is always there,

Like waves crashing

Into the stillness.

Hope

'When I be a grown-up Mummy,

I want to be a Daddy.'

'When I be a grown-up Mummy,

I'm going to marry you'.

When you are a grown-up,

Mummy will be proud of you.

Mummy will hold you tight,

And be with you,

Hopefully too.

The invitation

I didn't know what to say

When the invite came in.

'Any dietary requirements?'

How do I relay this?

'Parents can drop off'

I need to stay.

I'm careful in what I say,

I want more invites to come.

A chance for you to be treated

Just like

Anyone.

The gathering continued

Two have left now,

It's an achievement.

Yet, it leaves me with tears,

That little thought creeps in,

Why do others get to keep their child?

Why am I left with this agonising pain?

But two less professionals,

Is an achievement

right?

No rest

There are times when there is too much,

If you were to get a hold of yourself,

It would be too much.

Too much fear,

Too many what ifs,

There is no rest.

You can put it aside from time to time,

But it is always lurking,

Waiting for you to remember it.

Sensory memory

Did I wipe the toothbrush dry?

Before I gave it to you?

Did I remember?

Did I pick up the clothes with my wet hands?

Before I gave them to you?

Did I remember?

Did I check the seams of the socks?

Before I put them on you?

Did I remember?

Did I forget you prefer your collar under your
jumper?

Mummy didn't remember.

Bedtime

It's 7.31pm,

We started winding down 31 minutes ago.

Your anxiety is at an all-time high,

Your routine is different,

I'm riding the storm that has taken your anchor.

'Please put your pjs on.'

It falls deaf on your ears,

You are rolling on the floor,

Trying to get some input,

Anything.

You are lining up objects,

You are doing *anything* that isn't putting on your pyjamas.

You are rolling your tongue,

Singing a song,

Crashing into furniture,

Anything that isn't putting on your pyjamas.

There's a glimmer of hope... I help with your jumper,

But you don't like the feeling of it over your
head,

We go again,

Rolling

Crashing

Anything that isn't putting on your pyjamas.

So, I sit, and I wait,

As I know in a moment,

The switch will flip.

The pyjamas will go on,

And you will cuddle me so tight,

That what has just happened,

Feels like it didn't at all.

Fear

I live with a fear,

A fear, so intense

That at times the simplest question

Triggers the tears.

The thoughts coming running in,

My mind is defenceless,

All I can think of is my fear.

Unique

I am but here nor there,

Nor somewhere in between.

I haven't happened yet,

No one knows how to treat me,

Or have a cure for me.

I am researched,

Tested,

And yet, they are none the wiser.

I'll do me,

I'll live my own path,

I'll guide others,

Maybe even inspire the doubters.

Thank you to everyone who is continuing to support our family. The compassion we have received is overwhelming.

Printed in Great Britain
by Amazon

81713627R00040